Piano · Vocal · Guitar

CRAZY HEART

Music from the Motion Picture Soundtrack

ISBN 978-1-4234-7769-3

HAL•LEONARD® CORPORATION

7777 W. BLUEMOUND RD. P.O. BOX 13819 MILWAUKEE, WI 53213

Visit Hal Leonard Online at
www.halleonard.com

(To Get A)
HOLD ON YOU

Written by STEPHEN BRUTON,
T BONE BURNETT, JOHN GOODWIN
and BOB NEUWIRTH

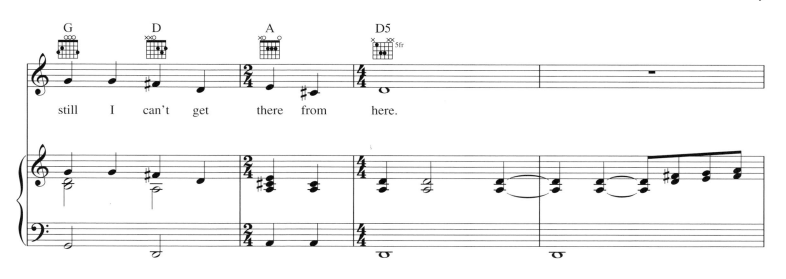

still I can't get there from here.

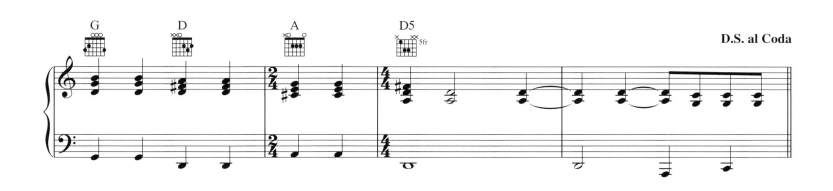

D.S. al Coda

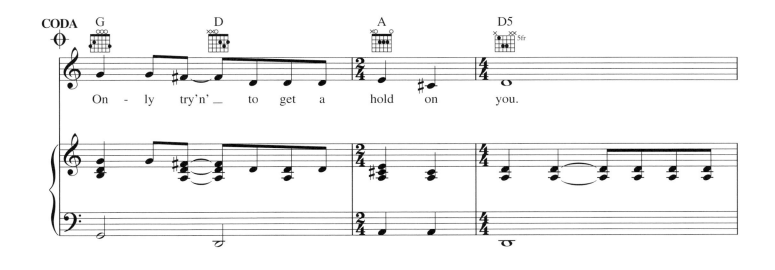

CODA

On - ly try'n'__ to get a hold on you.

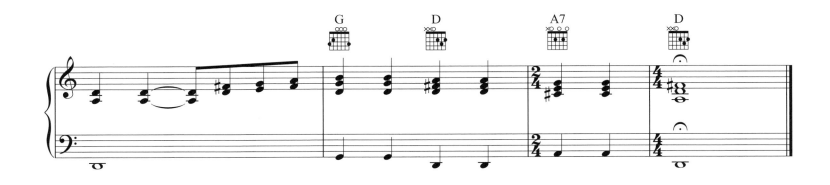

HELLO TROUBLE

Words and Music by EDDIE McDUFF
and ORVILLE COUCH

Recorded a half step higher.

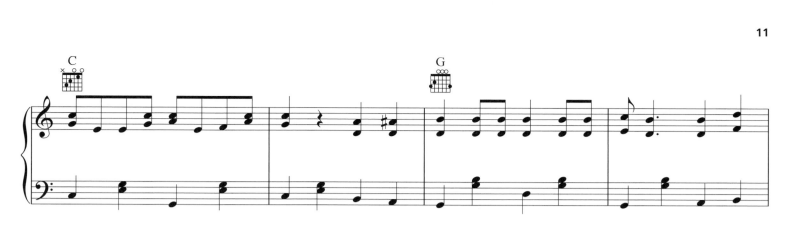

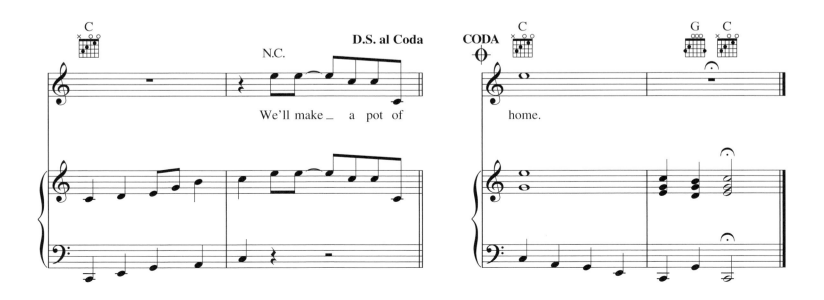

We'll make _ a pot of

home.

MY BABY'S GONE

Words and Music by
HAZEL HOUSER

SOMEBODY ELSE

Written by STEPHEN BRUTON
and T BONE BURNETT

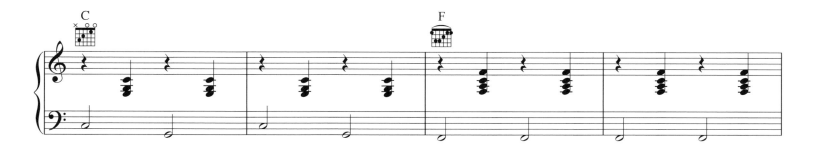

I DON'T KNOW

Written by STEPHEN BRUTON
and T BONE BURNETT

Moderately

I don't know, _ ba-by, where we stand. _ Where's the fu - ture

that we planned _ so long a - go?

I don't know. ___

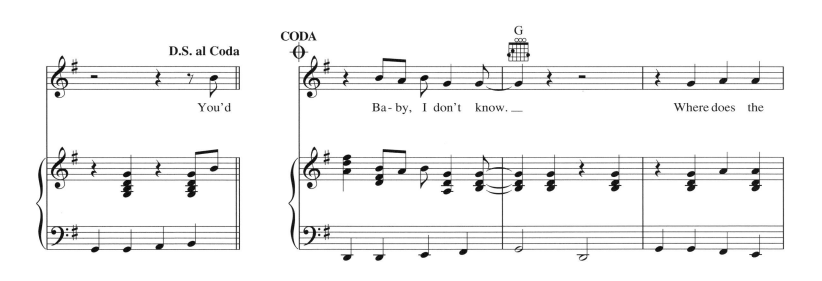

D.S. al Coda

CODA

You'd

Ba- by, I don't know. ___

Where does the

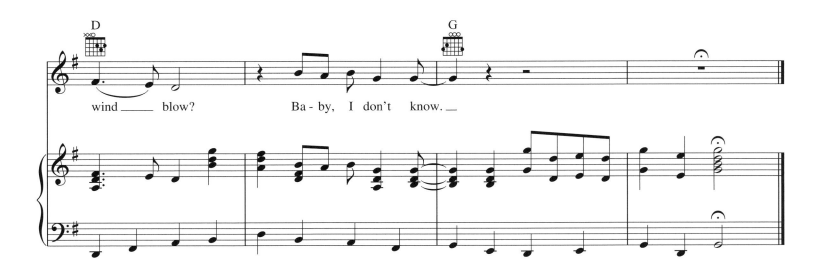

wind ___ blow?

Ba- by, I don't know. ___

ONCE A GAMBLER

Written by
SAM HOPKINS

1. Yeah, you know I once was a gamb-ler,
2.-4. *(See additional lyrics)*
but I lost __ my mon-ey roll.

Yeah, you know I once was a gam-bler,

but I lost __ my mon-ey roll.

That's the rea-son I don't have

no sweet wom - an. ____ Now I done lost my hap - py home. _

Additional Lyrics

2. You take a gambler and when he lose that no good money,
   He sat around with his head hung down.
   When you lose that ol' dog gone money,
   You'll sit around with your head hung down.
   You'll try to borrow you fifty dollars
   To start all over again in another town.

3. Baby, if you only will forgive me,
   I won't gamble no more.
   If you only will forgive me, baby,
   Ol' Lightnin' won't gamble no more.
   She says I can't help you now.
   Sold out to the devil and that's no way to go.

4. She said I didn't want you to gamble, Lightnin'.
   You know who I am - I'm your wife.
   She said I didn't want you to gamble, Lightnin'.
   You know who I am - I am your wife.
   She said lookee here brother, just like you lost your money,
   You had a good chance to lose your life.

FALLIN' & FLYIN'

Words and Music by STEPHEN BRUTON
and GARY NICHOLSON

I was go-in' where I should-n't go,
tired of be-in' good.

And start-ed see-in' who I should-n't see,
miss-in' that ol' feel-in' free.

Stopped

It all hap - pens for a rea - son e - ven

when it's wrong, __ es - pe - cial - ly when it's

wrong. _____

ARE YOU SURE HANK DONE IT THIS WAY

Words and Music by
WAYLON JENNINGS

Lord, it's the same old tune, fid - dle and gui - tar.

Where do we take it from here? Rhine - stone suits and

new shin - y cars, __ it's been the same way for years.

Recorded a half step higher.

30

GONE, GONE, GONE

Written by T BONE BURNETT,
STEPHEN BRUTON and RYAN BINGHAM

Moderately fast

I was born _____ on a flat top _____ two lane. Picked up a gui- -tar and ev-'ry day _____ I'd sing, well I _____ was

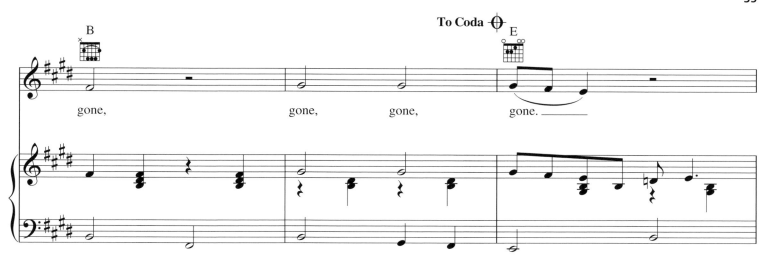

gone,   gone,   gone,   gone. _____

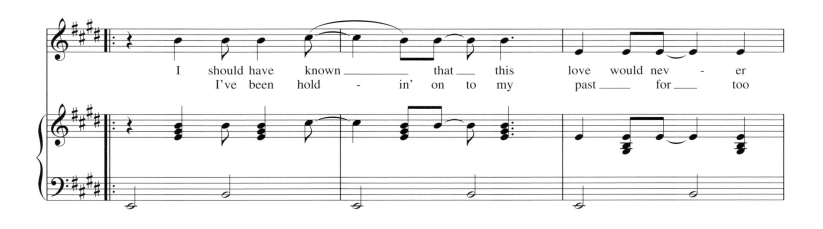

I should have known _____ that _____ this love would nev - er

I've been hold - in' on to my past _____ for _____ too

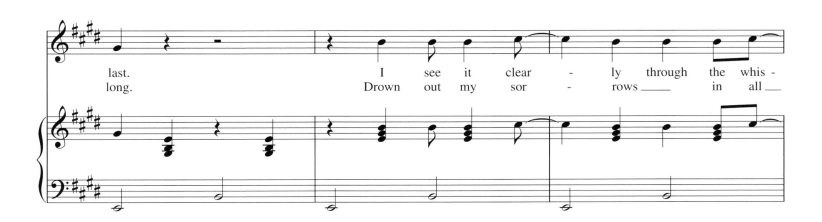

last.   I see it clear - ly through the whis -

long.   Drown out my sor - rows _____ in all _____

IF I NEEDED YOU

Written by
TOWNES VAN ZANDT

* Recorded a half step higher.

REFLECTING LIGHT

Words and Music by
SAM PHILLIPS

Now that I've worn out, I've worn out the world,

I'm on my knees in fas - ci - na - tion, look - ing through the

night. And the moon's nev - er seen me be -

LIVE FOREVER

Words and Music by BILLY JOE SHAVER
and EDDY SHAVER

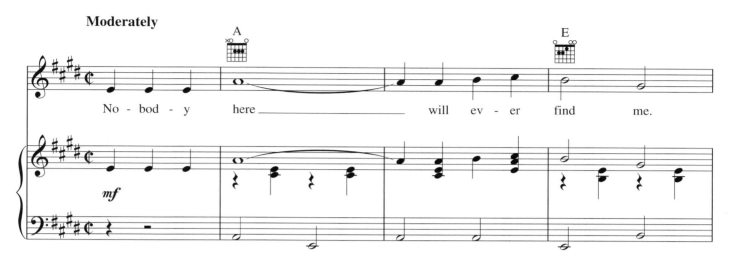

Moderately

No-bod-y here _____ will ev-er find me.

I'll al-ways be a-round.

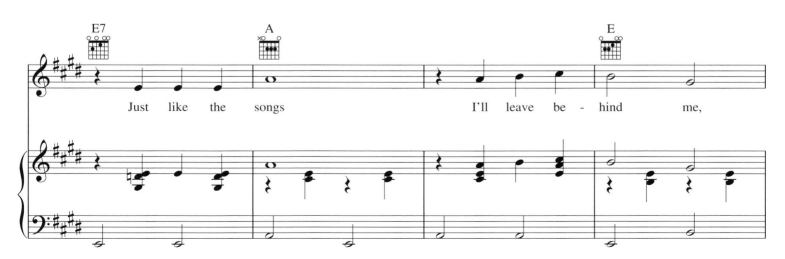

Just like the songs I'll leave be-hind me,

BRAND NEW ANGEL

Words and Music by
GREG BROWN

THE WEARY KIND
(Theme from CRAZY HEART)

Written by T BONE BURNETT
and RYAN BINGHAM

Moderately fast

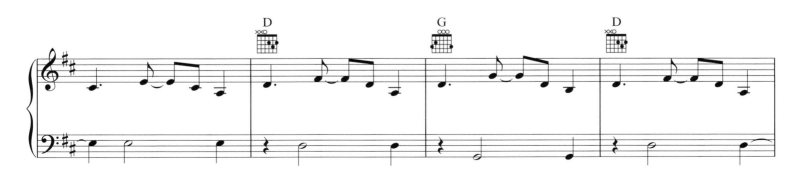